Little Anodynes

1/15/16

Dear Sam,

This poet is Pinoy. You will probably enjoy his work.

Love, Uncle Joel

THE PALMETTO POETRY SERIES
NIKKY FINNEY, SERIES EDITOR
KWAME DAWES, FOUNDING EDITOR

Little Anodynes

POEMS

Jon Pineda

Foreword by Oliver de la Paz

The University of South Carolina Press

Published by the University of South Carolina Press
Columbia, South Carolina 29208

www.sc.edu/uscpress

Manufactured in the United States of America

24 23 22 21 20 19 18 17 16 15
10 9 8 7 6 5 4 3 2 1

Library of Congress Cataloging-in-Publication Data
can be found at http://catalog.loc.gov/

ISBN 978-1-61117-525-7 (paperback)
ISBN 978-1-61117-526-4 (ebook)

This book was printed on recycled paper with
30 percent postconsumer waste content

For my family

The heart asks pleasure first,
And then excuse from pain;
And then, those little anodynes
That deaden suffering

Emily Dickinson

Contents

Foreword

Over the past ten years, Jon Pineda has been writing poems of aching grace. Intimately he draws the reader into the embrace of his language, at once quiet and tender, then suddenly surging with the arresting violence of a childhood marred by intolerance, loneliness, and regret. I use the term "embrace" because the idea persists that touch, either tender or terrible, is a means toward human understanding. Memory and the pain of loss are at the core of his poetic dilemmas, starting with *Birthmark* and continuing with *The Translator's Diary*. In each of those earlier works, Pineda attempted to reconcile the death of his sister, the tyranny of coming-of-age, and the responsibility of fatherhood. Through it all Pineda clearly works within the most difficult of mediums—the complex and distinctly individualized space of human suffering. In his poetic endeavor to bridge the differences between us, the past collapses into moments of wisdom and understanding, consoling us through their beauty.

The poems in his latest collection, *Little Anodynes,* are a continuation of Jon Pineda's generous, meditative, and immediate genius. Like the title of the book, derived from Emily Dickinson's "Poem 536," the poems within bring us salves for our suffering. The poems are written in breathless ribbons of prose verse, where moments from youth collapse into epiphanies fired from the synapses. In the first poem of the book, "First Concert," the speaker describes the experience of attending his first concert, declaring:

                                    . . . I
want   to   believe   I   was
learning   something   about
the world on the car ride
home   my   friend   &   I
punched   each   other   we
didn't know how to feel so
we   took   it   out   on   one
another . . .

And in the adrenalized first understandings of the world, the small
surges of pain delivered by fists are akin to the first articulations
of self. The understanding of what it means to be in one's skin, the
bruises left behind. Later the boy encounters his sister before her
tragic automobile accident, awaiting his return from the concert, and
an older speaker thinks back on this small moment:

                         . . . in another
year   a   car   accident   would
take   away   this   version   of
her   sometimes   I   like   to   go
back   to   this   brief   moment
in the hallway the two of us
there   sharing   what   we   both
knew   &   would   never   know

From this vantage point, the speaker's mind is turning and turning
in on itself in unpunctuated and breathless ribbons of reverie. This
is the bruise that will not heal. That will never heal. And, in looking
back at this small eruption of memory, the versions of the self are
ghostly images spliced into an ever-turning reel of film.

    In a later poem, "Spectators," Pineda again finds the place where
the boy in the process of understanding himself encounters the

extravagant beauty of the world and its conflicts. This time the older speaker is watching a Miguel Cotto versus Manny Pacquiao boxing match with his son and they are delighting in the ballet of violence:

> . . . we hit play on the DVR &
> mapped   how   Pacquiao's
> gloves   pressed   into   the
> statistics   they   would   taking
> their   place   in   the   fate   of   the
> other   boxer's   face   *Man*   we
> whispered in unison on cue . . .

Both father and son interject *"Man,"* framing themselves within the violence of Pacquiao's pinpoint jabs—their own masculinities in full display as the bodies of two men collide in a violent spectacle. They both seem to delight in Cotto's pummeling until the poem's end, when the speaker again enters to reframe the moment:

> . . . I let the match go
> on   though   only   fast
> forwarding   to   spots   where
> Cotto   fell   the   fighter's   own
> son   finally   escorted   away
> from   the   ring   ours   tapping
> his spoon like a bell

The pleading of Cotto's son for the fight's end while being pulled away from the ring marks the speaker as culpable in a theater of brutality to which there is no salve, save the father's own recognition of this human dilemma. Like the previous poem, the past is gathered and then reorganized into a single image that remains within the frame—a still point amid the ever-moving currents of the speaker's remembrances.

And, like the father and son witnessing the spectacle of a boxing match, the speaker later bears witness to the aftermath of a friend's suicide in the title poem, "Little Anodynes." In the poem the speaker is teaching his son to ride a bicycle; the recollection of a friend who has passed haunts this idyllic moment:

>   . . . later
> the   night   sky   will   appear
> &   always   will   have   my
> friend   still   studying   the   thin
> small   mouth   of   a   barrel
> the   cold   beauty   of   it   *One*
> *by   one   the   stars   go   out—*
> a   world   no   longer   held
> within   language   I   should
> have   looked   away   stared
> at   the   trees   &   listened   for
> signs   of   joy   as   he   rode   off
> it   would   make   a   better
> story   but   I   chase   after   him
> *Don't*   *let   me   go*
> he   says   laughing   when
> I realize I already have

Like the poems mentioned before this one, physical contact—touch—is the tether between the present and the past. The brutality of a boxing match, the playful jabs between young boys, even the steadying guidance of a father's hand on a son's bicycle—all are gestures in a journey toward a profound intimacy between the speaker and the reader.

From the resulting intersection, skin on skin, memory on memory, and sentence sliding into sentence, we find, as Frost wrote, "momentary stay[s] against confusion." Within these "little anodynes /

that deaden suffering," we find ourselves, always reaching for some-one else—someone who may be right next to us or someone from our deep paths. Regardless of the distance, in *Little Anodynes,* Jon Pineda's resolute and lyrical language traverses the spectrum of human conditions and eases our lonely and troubled selves into the possibility of joy.

OLIVER DE LA PAZ

One

First Concert

In   front   of   us   were
teenagers with shoe polish
black   mohawks   passing
a joint back & forth one
with hair pulled into nails
glistering with gelatin then
the lights went down & we
could feel Lee Rocker's bass
lines filling our chests our
hearts   pulled   taut   &
plucked amplified I was
a small kid eleven years old
&   unsure   grinning   with
a   contact   buzz   then   my
friend   nudged   me   &
pointed again we followed
the glowing speck as it spun
landed on lips brightening
for a sec then lost in smoke
Brian   Setzer   skinny   &
tattooed was all sleeveless
snarl   his   tempered
crooning   slinging   his
glittery   electric   hollow

body he strummed &
stamped his buckled boots
the stage looking slick with
sweat & colored lights I
want to believe I was
learning something about
the world on the car ride
home my friend & I
punched each other we
didn't know how to feel so
we took it out on one
another the lights on
the Hampton Roads Bridge
Tunnel ticked by combing
through the interior of
the Cadillac I would look up
& see my friend's father
nodding to the music on
the radio his gray mop
of hair swatting at
the stretched cloth of
the ceiling strands stood on
end like an orb of electricity
one of those glass balls you
might find crackling with
small neon lightning in
a novelty store-front
window my friend punched
me in the stomach &
laughed we scrambled into
the trough of the floorboard
I returned the gesture this

4

was 1982 when I got home
my sister was standing in
the hallway with her arms
folded in front of her she
took one look at me & said
You're high then laughed
quietly & went back in her
room where the walls were
covered in teen magazine
poster pullouts in another
year a car accident would
take away this version of
her sometimes I like to go
back to this brief moment
in the hallway the two of us
there sharing what we both
knew & would never know

Prayer

We found ourselves gone
into the crowd on Bourbon
Street a river with its
current of tourists breaking
the invisible levees until
certain things drew us in
someone's wife undressed
among college students
quick to drape camera
flashes across her skin &
the man struggling to cover
her with his wrinkled suit
coat is her sad husband you
imagine his smile appears
as only an apology it is
almost January & the wind
lingering in the harsh
distance moves across
the marsh grass gathers
to speak its name over
the woman's nipples
sharpening while people

nearby   disappear   into
themselves it is an easier
descent among the alley-
ways lining the empty
church its rusted grate
meshed with the stench
of piss & blood how we all
emerged then into Jackson
Square the Baby about to
drop & signal the end of one
year the beginning of
another finding a spot
within the crowd your hand
holding onto your wife's
you feel there is always
a hint of sadness that hangs
back from any considerable
joy & waits your mother's
sure words like a prayer
through life *Remember*
laughter turns to crying
before the hour slides into
place you decide you will
cherish the temporal
holding onto each other's
face to steady yourselves
before the embrace of
the moment passes on you
enjoy a kiss among
the crowd of others

cheering through jazz &
blues drunk on Hurricanes

Outside   in   the   sun
a Louisiana winter hums
within bristled palms you
overhear someone a table
away say *Filipino Necktie* &
swipe   a   single   fingertip
across their throat others
among them laugh & it is
gruesome you think how
silence   then   follows
it settles over the food set
before them a woman's slim
fingers slide over the neck
of an opened bottle which
she struggles with a few
jolts to release the ketchup
its dimpled redness spills
onto her plate of fries &
catfish & when you return
to the conversation among
your   friends   they   are
smiling casually in their
hunger to be understood
the lull having gathered
about you all you want to
tell them a story about your
father one he'd waited until
you were grown to inherit
how when he was young

stationed in Norfolk a few
of the Filipinos from his
ship would spend week-
ends at a dancehall in
Ocean View & many times
over nights would end with
white sailors starting fights
with them those young
Filipinos in their custom-
made Hong Kong suits slick
as snakeskin their black
hair primed with pomade
they had to know they were
dangerous for girls would
come those nights wanting
only to dance with them &
so one night your father
says before the dance those
young Filipinos fashioned
thick chain links around
their necks under silk shirts
metal pressed heavily
against their skin & covered
marks left by a mother's
rosary when white sailors
cut in with their worn
routine of violence your
father continues smiling as
if he wasn't there *Those
Filipinos pulled off their
chains & began swinging
them at the other sailors'*

9

legs the music then had
stopped & the only sound it
seemed   to   him   was
the popping of bone into
the void where faces of
those girls wide-eyed have
long since vanished

Notes for a Memoir

In my research I found
the name of the young man
who drove a dump truck
filled with warm sand
it was just one day
the way he carried
the small burden before
touching the car a window
pressed my sister's raised
hand

Strawberries

Newborn Luke rests on
my chest downstairs you
rummage the dark for
the breast pump the
refrigerator door opens
with a quick sucking sound
because our house is small
I hear this   know by now
you must have found those
blood red strawberries in
a bowl I'd placed inside on
the glass shelf I lean
as close to him as I can
I smell you on his breath
then a knife slides deep into
the sink its blade even wet
sounds against the skin
of rubbed porcelain cast
iron fresh rust   I think of
the man my son will
become & kiss him softly
on the mouth

Ceiling & Ground

Our docent of limestone
a local boy hums nudges
the air where a glazed
column has grown together
there stalactites verge on
stalagmites emerged from
a pool of milky blue water
Amy whispers to me "It's
easier if you just remember
c is for *ceiling* & *g* is for
ground" I push the stroller
she holds Luke's hand
within our group of land
dwellers we descend
farther into the main
chamber it is a slow spiral
downward all must
negotiate the slick decline
at one point our young
guide's voice breaks as he
beckons beyond the guard
railing says "Over there's
Pluto's Chasm" & goes on to
explain how it doesn't end

or at least from what we
can tell it sinks through
itself in a moment of
collective awe for the god
of the underworld it is then
our daughter removes
the pacifier from her mouth
& hurls this most
prized possession into
the precious abyss I wish
I could say it didn't happen
shocked the group then
continues on & we parents
of an irreverent soul follow
bowing our heads though
embarrassed I'm secretly
pleased I know Amy is as
well since she asks
the guide if they ever have
to clean out these caverns
the boy pauses looking for
the right words I don't envy
him nor the one he explains
must be lowered with ropes
& harness searching
the dark for those
unfortunate signs of life

Collectors

We search along the shore
for bits of sea glass amber &
green   pieces   blinking
among   broken   shells
the ocean is too cold for
wading   &   so   each   time
waves wash up shore break
fades into moons crescents
our   daughter   screams   &
rushes with bucket sloshing
about   fear   lost   when   she
smiles for me or for her
brother   our   burgeoning
surgeon   already   busily
sliding   some   driftwood
across   the   prismed   belly
of   a   jellyfish   sea   glass
frosts over when it dries
sides   mostly   smooth
pocked   from   the   nearly
endless tumbling of its life
arriving during low tide it is
no   longer   a   shard
not wine or beer bottle no

longer one of those clear
ones that might have held
a model of a Spanish
galleon maybe even of
Magellan's when he sailed
into the shoals of Mactan
before Lapu Lapu's men
found him a grave this little
ship in history its sails
on the miniature rolled like
tiny scrolls fastened with
thread could just have
easily been palimpsest or
parchment on which some-
one had written one
message over and again—
*Love   don't stop looking for
me*   in Corolla we gather
what we can find & head
back to the hotel where she
calls to us from above on
the balcony each of us will
lift our hands to present
blinking trinkets what we
had found on the beach
seems pulled from a shared
dream no discretion in our
joy—Emma screams again
when Luke rushes to show
his findings first garbled
mole crabs marbled dark
blue of an oyster's half shell

lapping among his sure
hands like the tongue of
a Chow mix we once owned
but later had to put to sleep
our *Lucy Goose* & now
Emma pushing Luke aside
smiling in triumph as only
his little sister is allowed
the mermaid's purse this
small thing she relishes & it
looks more like something
scorched remnant of a blaze
more paper-like than
puffed black egg pouch it
doesn't really matter
though we're collectors
proud of the things we
carry home with us in red
plastic buckets

Silence

And if I tell no one,
Will something live on inside my silence.

Larry Levis

I don't remember what she
named it so it's better this
way   the   nameless   joy
my sister the oldest had
held onto more than once
before returning it to its
prison of plywood & wire
faded hay I remember its
droppings were round like
little   planets   they
resembled   toppled
pyramids fallen stones of
the ancient structures lost
in the ground's straw lattice
when our father had left on
deployment   older   boys   in
the   neighborhood   would
come   around   tapping
crooked   thumbs   against

the storm windows anxious
I'd awoken one morning to
find the house dark the rest
of the world content to
dream I pulled on
dungarees patches our
mother had sewn on knees
& wrenched my head
through the neck of a jersey
I'd made *All Stars* that
summer before my fingers
now catching on stray laces
of my Chucks I walked
outside to first light to feed
the rabbit whose name
I must have known then
whispered it on the way
calling to its cage until I
found what could have been
the heart its flesh
a brownish red spread like
a dough across the dusted
grass the longer I stared
I couldn't help thinking
it might rise this deflated
ball to become a piece of
nebula spanning the gray
foot another in the distance
more scraps of fur some
burst of white then its small
silly head the eyes were
frozen each a pale yellow

twin suns in the universe of
our dead lawn I felt like
a little god mischievous
with my catcher's hands
ungloved & nervous
choking up on the shovel I
paused each time I brought
the blade to the dirt
connecting with clay I
smacked the earth trying
to assemble the animal &
instead remade this anger
years later I think of those
boys & of her yet to wake
unchanged by it all together

Two

The Ocean

I wait for my name
in the house our son will
call for me when he wakes
I know standing at the top
of the stairs in a daze
the morning before we'd
stood near the shore
porpoises corralled a school
of blues by slapping their
tails against the gray
surface all in a circle until
there was the ocean now
just the current of a story
our son wants to relay
I climb the steps & lift him
up his ear the perfect shell
small & damp intact with
subtle curves cartilage
we share with the sharks
when he leans close I
almost hear the ocean there
inside us all

Sealed Letter

Weeks we waited for a letter
from him my father on
deployment in the Med
then one evening early with
the dusk calming our yard
we thought we heard
the blatant scrape of metal
on metal as a shadow slid
the barrel a 12-gauge across
our wiry fence it wedged our
dog's head against burnt
orange grass all an animal
I'd never seen before our
dog contorted held in
whimpering by my neighbor
intent to kill his own were
pinned up *in heat* ours had
gone under the fence to find
release I recall I whispered
Dear God—

She appeared urgent with
her purse tucked under an
arm I followed her slowly to

where she ended searching
through contents until she
paused & in one it seemed
practiced   gesture   brought
out the pistol to the man's
head he winced as if stung
suddenly a bright snub nose
rubbed his trembling temple
I swear my mother didn't
care who saw her do such
a thing there was one law &
then another   she spoke
without saying anything or
maybe she did all words for
the body of this sealed letter
the one never sent

There Is an Edge to Each Image

Years after they were first
set loose in Central Park
starlings   disappear   into
silhouettes of gray hulls
culled together by cranes in
the   sleepless   shipyard
if there is an edge to each
image the light will find it
as   it   finds   a   woman
gathering her things on
a bench overlooking this
bend   in   the   Elizabeth
across the river an evening
sun fills the façade of
the   naval   hospital   in
Portsmouth   with   broad
strokes   of   ochre
the   building's   vacant
windows   seem   to   her
a signal of something lost
almost futile now a memory
tugging at her hand as if

a small child when she
remembers the moment it
is of her son years ago lifted
onto a gurney so that
a young corpsman could
sew together a gash in the
child's foot it was
the corpsman's first time
his hands shook slightly as
he threaded the eye of
the bright needle with
coarse black string her son
had been out roaming
the neighboring woods
when a glass shard angled
just so in soft mud had
chosen him it would be
this way forever oblivious
the boy lay quietly & stared
into one of the walls gray
surrounding them all while
his mother sitting close
to him forced herself to
become lost within
the mending within this
wound

Distance

Before the hillsides forced
us underground we thought
one burden might have
been a lost lullaby in
the gull's song we thought
ourselves untouched by
a child rummaging in
the heap remnants for
building the story of
survival we thought
the noise in the distance
was not so much dynamite
thrown into the ocean as it
was the same ocean given
over to its grief the way
the sound of waves might
be mistaken for sadness we
thought we heard dogs
digging as the child digs to
reach a source hidden
where the air is untouched
where breathing is we can
say this now not at all like
breathing

Ellipses

We race each other up
the hill the grass slick
where others have
ascended before us it is
a steep incline overlooking
a man-made space on
which speckled geese
obscure themselves turning
away to drift into
the distant shore ending at
Independence Boulevard
within an interval of cars
these ellipses I explain
the origin of this hill how it
was before anything else an
open land fill she pats my
hand motions for me to
return to bend down so that
she can read my face
she runs through a catalog
things for possible trash
then laughs *Even dirty
diapers? Yes* I say *even those
Gross* she says & I wonder

where she learned this
word *But look,* I say, *how
pretty this place is* farther
down the plateau a boy
holds a spool everything
invisible above him until we
see the blue & yellow kite
its tail a spine of red
triangles leaves a blurry
trail in the sky *What about
those?* she says & I look in
the direction of her
pointing her small wrist
twirling until I finally see all
is buried underneath our
short-lived joy

My Place

When it is late let me recall
my daughter's laughter &
the   story   she   will
remember for her mother
both whispering as if I'm
not standing there among
them the two pretend to
share again the surprise of
joy in the relaying of this
story I realize my place
my silence coaxes again
the   saw   grass   divides
the air so as not to disrupt
light falling into a small
tunnel here the crab is
nearly translucent unreal
were it not for those
eyes   buttons fastened to
the beige cloth of its smooth
body Emma & Luke watch it
climb up into the shadow of
them both crouching to
study its ascent through
sliding sand & me wanting

more for my children finally
slipping off one of my
Chucks to scoop the thing &
show how easily it is done
setting something free

Three

We Left the Camera

On   in   the   ocean   fish
at once filled the frame so
that it did not appear there
was water to consider just
some pixelated lookdowns
silvering an entombed image

Ritual

Some mornings I pretend to
sleep our room cool as
a tomb before the radiator
has jeweled the air to weigh
us further into the next life
& that is usually when she
arrives   stuffed   animals
she places on either side of
us a dog named *Tickle* &
a   cat   whose   name   I
have   forgotten   in   your
slumbering you are almost
a sarcophagus while she is
already   whispering
the ritual the play by play of
her prayer what is what &
what goes where content
she then climbs between us
rests her hands on our faces
until the moment is little
more   than   what   it   is
returning those awake in
the   temporary   temple
of Love's making

Edenton

There was a secret about
the house wasps dropped
onto figs busted skins
light fell in sheets across
Silver Queen my uncle
primed the rusted pump
we rummaged fallen slats
the metal roof a thin brush
of paint over brittle tin

The Story

She only learned the story
from him before he was
ever married when his life
still held within itself
numerous things yet to
come rife he sat among
sailors as they passed
around a revolver one
would spin the tiny silver
wheel which held inside
a tiny seed the one brutally
true thing each time
my father made the
hammer *click* the others
would cheer I want to think
it was for me he held his
breath though of course he
wouldn't for one second
have known me then
waiting on the other side of
his surrendering

It Is Simple

He walks the driveway back
to the house the mail
something he will look
through at the table it is
quiet on this side of Mobile
the   lands   divided
subdivided it is only now &
then a plane might fly
nearby enough to remind
anyone of the places they've
been or the people they've
lost but never mind what is
sad that will come now is
the scent of garlic on
fingers as he opens a letter
from Italy & finds no note
only pieces to a puzzle the
father shakes from an
envelope on the stove
chicken   adobo   juices
cooking into layers of meat
until it is all the same color
like coffee without milk
the way the son has learned

to drink it in Florence
where times he has paused
along the Ponte Santa
Trinita the Arno clouded
after a storm & thought of
him on one side of the
puzzle a few letters half
of a word & on the other
laminated colors to
a painting the father spends
an afternoon putting
together at the kitchen
table again the scent of
garlic on each piece & then
it is done the father turns
the picture of the bridge
over & finds a message his
son has written it is simple
a phrase in Tagalog
the language between them

Spectators

I   saved   the   Cotto   fight
for   my   son   to   watch
I poured   another   cup   of
coffee   while   he   brought
Lucky Charms into the living
room & there early morning
we hit play on the DVR &
mapped   how   Pacquiao's
gloves   pressed   into   the
statistics they would taking
their place in the fate of the
other boxer's face *Man* we
whispered in unison on cue
Amy & Emma   still   asleep
upstairs I let the match go
on   though   only   fast
forwarding to spots where
Cotto fell the fighter's own
son   finally   escorted   away
from the ring ours tapping
his spoon like a bell

Kundiman

Kazim pauses to glimpse
what we both feel is Icarus
the others rush ahead of us
all morning cardinals build
themselves into magnolias
a stranger says to another
*There's no one way to get
there* across the Grounds
an empty bus rounds
a loggia of trees as blue
melts into the light
blue hills of Charlottesville

Trailer

There are burn marks
where the floor is concave
the green carpet melted as
if from ashtrays overturned
the contents mashed we
play in the trailer & avoid
this spot later we'll run
outside & pull the thin
metal apron away & peer
underneath see the bowed
flooring giving more from
this view no one says not to
& so we think it's okay to
scurry there when we come
out the other side my
uncle's bakery truck is idle
in the gravel we want
nothing more than to climb
inside years later I climb
the steps & listen as this
new structure echoes
within the bell tower
I reach the metal grate &

look out onto the country-
side beyond the old walls of
San   Gimigniano   I   don't
know why I study the plat-
form   where   I'm   standing
but I do until slivers align
with   each   successive   one
below segments fit into an
image   that's   when
the ground floor bursts up
through the grate & washes
over me it is film pulled taut
on the projector the clicking
sounds falling away into the
transition   of   a   scene
the vertigo is startling its
suddenness then even more
so the thought that it had
been   waiting   so   patiently
inside me it will be years
before I'll know the word
trailer   also   refers   to
promotional   footage
a glimpse at the film yet
to be released until then
I will visit Cinecitta & take
note of a huge fake boulder
leftover from a Stallone film
I make it a point not to see
that movie when it comes
out   instead   I   will   sit   in
a   dark   classroom   near

the   Arno   screening
Spaghetti   Westerns
featuring   a   young   Clint
Eastwood   &   know   that
except for him everyone in
the scene is speaking Italian
I wanted to dream in this
language my first week in
Florence I approach a street
vendor & tell her I'd like to
buy   a   *fish*   she   looks
confused   but   then   nods
smiling & hands me a *peach*
I offer my ten-year old son
this   story   &   he   laughs
he remembers the twist at
the end but lets me tell
the   story   anyway   his
younger   sister   is   in
the other room sitting at
the computer   she wants
to learn Tagalog my father's
language she has a program
to help her   all three of us
use it off & on she calls out
to us now *Tatlo, dalawa,*
isa? I let the inflection live
inside   my   head   for
a moment I know she is
asking us what the words
mean   *Three* her brother
answers   quickly   *two   one*

I think of the numbers on
a flickering screen a thin
straight line attached at
the center of each numeral
spirals clockwise they are
counting down before the
film begins it is here that
I want to go back to that
moment on my uncle's
truck there are little
pastries filled with custard
some with fruit glaze
*Peaches   Pesche   Mga
milokoton* they are covered
in a translucent wax paper
stamped with the bakery's
red oval logo in the trailer
of this memory the pastries
are still warm as if just
pulled from the oven
they are not stale or past
their expiration dates &
they were never going to be
thrown away to never be
thought of again

Umpteenth

Remind me I was pissed
getting up from the table to
stand there at the foot of
the stairs Emma calling me
for the umpteenth time
stalling before sleep this
back & forth ritual this
game we had played before
remind me that my poem
unfinished in the journal
I left open was unimportant
was nothing only jibber
jabber was line after line
a forced lyric rain fell
against the windows of our
children's one room &
Emma kept calling me
to say she was scared *Yes?*
I said & she repeated her
fear of the rain & I stupid
me would not climb
the stairs & hold her No
I thought we didn't do that
kind of thing anymore

instead I told her there was
nothing to be afraid of
that rain was a good sound
& that little girl there in
the dark called back to me
said *Okay*   then nothing
more so I returned to my
journal & erased what I had
written to ascend those
stairs again

Arrival

Or let the world remind you
the   letters   cast   within
the skin of a wrecking ball
the word it made blurring
walls waver like curtains in
an open window each room
folding   into   every   room
you've ever known a dead
letter office   nearby in
Monroe   Park   a   woman
gathers what little is left of
this one moment & feeds its
small stones into the mouth
of   a   stray   even   now
someone is writing to you
in the glittering smear of
night its disappearing ink
or the letter again unfolding
where one holds the page
out offering simple breath
to   script   breath   to

the longhand as if flourish
itself were tinder brushing
bright   then   diminishing
the letter meant nothing
before your arrival

Four

Little Anodynes

My friend's suicide waits
next to a memory of my son
at six learning to ride his
bicycle on campus at ODU
there too is his laughter
my son's when he turns
finds no one holding on
before him are the endless
paths to the ground he
could have taken I stood
in wonder watching him go
if a life could be reduced to
words let my friend's be
the line in a song a stranger
sings to herself while
crossing beyond Larchmont
the traffic builds on
Hampton Boulevard near
the bridge overlooking
the marina & the gaunt blue
silhouettes of Norfolk
International Terminals it is
evening it is always evening
& the words become an

affection the woman
harbors within gone inside
her like porpoises holding
their breath easily they
descend rhythmic singing
that fuses with the dark
syllables carry her across
not only this bridge but
elsewhere to the end of
summer into an autumn
when a Ferris Wheel might
appear in a field & light
the subdivisions nearby
let her walk in hand with
someone handsome past
temporary stalls filled with
those smiling animals all in
pastel & hanging by their
necks she will be reminded
of her youth Tuesday
Markets butchers' booths
gleaming with trinkets that
are instead the sun-glazed
skins of rabbits & farther
down where a stroll will
bring one closer to the Arno
the spot where Shelley
drafted long lines to
the West Wind gypsies
wait for those wandering
beyond the city but now
it is early enough to believe

wild rabbits killing lawns
in this one Norfolk morning
are little anodynes   as
are the etched hearts in
the wrinkled bark of pin
oaks here a rabbit rears
back on its hind legs an eye
glued to the air it acts like a
father to the others guards
the wavering space for
those still unaware that I'm
anywhere near a book
of poems tucked under an
arm but first my neighbor
must jog by as I've seen her
do what seems a thousand
times now & now her very
being is the rhythm in a line
I'd once read by the poet
Tu Fu—*One by one the stars
go out*   at her approach
rabbits scatter & later
the night sky will appear
& always will have my
friend still studying the thin
small mouth of a barrel
the cold beauty of it   *One
by one the stars go out*—
a world no longer held
within language I should
have looked away stared
at the trees & listened for

signs of joy as he rode off
it would make a better
story but I chase after him
Don't   let   me   go
he   says   laughing   when
I realize I already have

Acknowledgments

My thanks go to the editors of the following magazines, where many of these poems first appeared (and all in different versions): *CEllA's Roundtrip, Cerise Press, Collagist, Copper Nickel, Diode, Drunken Boat, Ecotone, maganda, minnesota review, MiPOesis: Asian American Issue, Pebble Lake Review,* and *Third Coast.*

A big round of hugs goes to my family and friends, Terra Chalberg, Nikky Finney, Jonathan Haupt, Joseph Legaspi, *KundimanKundiman Kundiman,* Oliver de la Paz, the M.F.A. program at Queens University of Charlotte, the University of Mary Washington, and the University of South Carolina Press.

About the Author

JON PINEDA was born in Charleston, South Carolina, and raised in Chesapeake, Virginia. The recipient of a Virginia Commission for the Arts Individual Artist Fellowship, Pineda is the author of the novel *Apology*, winner of the Milkweed National Fiction Prize and author of the memoir *Sleep in Me*, a Barnes & Noble "Discover Great New Writers" selection and a top memoir of 2010 by *Library Journal*. His poetry collections are *The Translator's Diary,* winner of the 2007 Green Rose Prize from New Issues Poetry & Prose, and *Birthmark*, selected by Ralph Burns as winner of the 2003 Crab Orchard Award Series open competition. An earlier version of *Little Anodynes* was a finalist for the National Poetry Series. Pineda teaches in the low-residency M.F.A. program at Queens University of Charlotte and at the University of Mary Washington. He lives in Virginia with his family.